Story-Writing Handbook

Written by Caroline Leavitt · Illustrated by Nancy Meyers

For information contact:
Mondo Publishing
980 Avenue of the Americas
New York, NY 10018
Visit our website at www.mondopub.com

Printed in China

09 10 11 12 13   PBK   9 8 7 6 5 4 3 2 1

ISBN 978-1-60201-977-5

Design by Witz End Design

CONTENTS

INTRODUCTION

The Stories in Our Lives

Why Do We Love Stories?

It's late at night. You and some friends are gathered around a crackling campfire, and everyone is taking turns telling ghost stories. The tales are so scary that the hair is prickling on the back of your neck. You can't wait until it's your turn to tell one (and boy, do you have a terrifying tale)!

Or maybe you're curled up on your favorite comfy chair on a rainy Saturday, reading a story about a boy who wakes up one morning on Mars. You're so lost in the adventure that you don't even hear the doorbell. When it rings again, it takes you a moment to realize you're not on Mars after all. You're in your own living room!

Or perhaps you're at the dining room table for a family feast. Great Aunt Karla is telling about the time she stowed away on a ship and sailed from Europe to the United States. Her story is amazing! You could feel that you were right on the ship with her, the deck rocking under your feet, salty air stinging your cheeks.

Why do we love stories? Maybe it's because wonderful stories take us away from our daily lives. They stretch our imaginations. We get to try on other lives for size. A good story can take us to another place, show us a way to solve a problem, or teach us something new about ourselves or others. Stories make us laugh, cry, reflect, and imagine.

There are all different types of stories. Stories are usually fiction, which means someone made them up. But they can be nonfiction, which means they are true, like Aunt Karla's story. In this handbook you're going to learn more about writing fiction stories. You'll discover how to get ideas. You'll learn how to create realistic characters. You'll see how to craft a plot, and why the right setting is so important. Putting words in your characters' mouths (the dialogue) can make your story come alive, and this book will give you some practice. Every story is constructed of certain elements; we'll help you figure out which part goes where—and why. Finally, you'll find a few suggestions for polishing and revising your story so it's just about perfect.

What Kind of Story Should You Write?

Where do ideas come from? Well, let's consider what kind of stories you like to read. Sometimes it's easier to write what you like or what you know. There are lots of different kinds. Sometimes they are referred to as different *genres* or *text types*. Here are some of them.

HISTORICAL FICTION You can read about the past in history books, but historical fiction can make history come alive in a different way. Usually the setting and some characters are real; they actually existed. Often the main character is made-up. For example, the *Dear America* series is written in the form of diaries of kids who "lived" during different periods in history. *Sounder*, by William H. Armstrong, tells about the hardships faced by a family of African American sharecroppers in the 19th century South. Historical fiction provides a "you-are-there" experience. If you love history and adventure, you might want to try writing historical fiction.

FANTASY When you think of fantasy, you probably think of wizards, dragons, castles, swordplay, and supernatural feats. J. K. Rowling's *Harry Potter* series is a great example of fantasy. Another is *Eragon* by Christopher Paolini—a wonderful story about dragon riders and the one boy who becomes the greatest dragon rider of all. The author wrote the first draft of this book when he was only 15! Fantasy, like historical fiction, takes you into a whole different world. But unlike historical fiction, it's a world that never existed. It probably never could! If you like to stretch your imagination, you may enjoy writing a fantasy.

SCIENCE FICTION Did you ever imagine that there might be a whole society of people (or creatures) living on Mars? Ever pretend you were the captain of a spacecraft bound for Jupiter? If so, you may want to try your hand at science fiction. This text type includes elements like robots, time travel, spaceships, and cool technology. Unlike fantasy, things that happen in science fiction *might* be possible in the future. Humans may not be visiting other planets yet, but scientists believe that we will some day. Robots are already part of our society— from little gizmos that clean our floors to robots that do medical experiments.

The Giver, by Lois Lowry, tells about a boy living in a futuristic society where there are lots of rules and no choices. He is chosen to be the Receiver of Memory for his society. These memories change his life and his feelings about his "perfect world." If you enjoy thinking about the amazing things the future may hold (and the problems that may arise) or thinking about life from a new perspective, science fiction might be fun to try.

MYSTERY It's just days before the big race, and someone has stolen your lucky sneakers! Who took them and why? Or maybe you were saving up for an MP3 player. Suddenly not only is the money gone, but there is also a note inside your money jar that reads: *Don't try to find me!* What's going on? It's a mystery! Mysteries are often called *whodunnits* because they are stories that raise questions like who committed the crime (*who done it?*) or what is the secret? For example, *Lily's Ghosts*, by Laura Ruby, revolves around a haunted house and a young girl who must solve the secrets of the past. The story moves back and forth between her life and the world of the ghosts who haunt the house. Can Lily find the secret and put her life—and the ghosts' existence—at peace? Part of the fun of a mystery is that it keeps you guessing. Sometimes authors of mysteries even plant fake clues, called *red herrings*, to deliberately throw you off. If you love puzzles, you just might want to write a mystery.

REALISTIC FICTION Do you sometimes feel as if no one else has the same problems that you have? Or that your family is crazier than any other family in town? Would your sister's babysitting adventures make a hilarious story? These would be realistic fiction—believable stories that can be funny, moving, or even sad and troubling. *My Last Best Friend,* by Julie Bowe, is about a girl who is sure that fourth grade will be NO FUN because her best friend has moved away. She's decided not to make a new best friend for fear of losing her, too. And yet—there's a new girl who seems really nice . . . . You can often identify with the dilemmas of the characters you're reading about in realistic fiction. Sometimes they have to solve problems that seem a lot like your own. Many authors encourage us to "write what we know." If you think that writing about everyday life might be enjoyable and maybe even useful, try writing some realistic fiction.

Thomas Edison once said that genius is one percent inspiration and ninety-nine percent perspiration. Lots of people feel that way about writing, too. Writing a great story isn't quick and easy. It is a process that requires hard work. But there are lots of ideas in this book that will help you. Now that you know more about the types of stories, let's talk a little about stories in general. In the next chapter, we'll break down what exactly makes a good story.

CHAPTER 1

What's the Story? A Few Basics

Getting Started

A story is really just a series of actions performed by a bunch of characters. Simple, right? But before you write a story, you need a plan. One good way to jump-start a story is to think of a "what if" situation. What if a kid stowed away on a spaceship? What if you woke up and suddenly had the power to see the future? What if your uncle could fly or change into any animal he wanted? Be as outlandish as you want—or as normal. What if you waited 15 minutes for the bathroom and your sister was *still* in the shower?

Another way is to think about your own life. Maybe you're shy. You might want to write a realistic story about a shy kid who really wants to try out for the school play, but who first has to gather enough courage just to go to the tryouts.

How will he or she manage to do that? What obstacles stand in the way, and how can they be overcome? Who helps? What is the outcome? Sounds like a great story!

Sometimes it helps to think of who, what, when, where, and why.

- WHO are the main characters?
- WHAT are they doing?
- WHEN is the story taking place?
- WHERE is the story taking place?
- WHY are the characters doing what they are doing?

You Try It!

Leaf through a magazine and find an interesting picture that shows people or animals doing something. It can be an athlete running the bases or diving into a pool. Maybe it's simply two people fighting or laughing or dancing. Or maybe it's a horse race. Try writing a brief story about the picture. Don't forget to consider who, what, when, where, why. Who are the characters? What are they doing and why? Where are they? What will happen next?

Now What?

Let's consider some basics. Every story has a beginning, a middle, and an end. The beginning introduces the main characters, the setting, and the main problem or conflict. The middle describes how the problem or conflict gets more and more complicated. Generally it reaches a climax, where the action gets super tense, and something's gotta give. The end is the solution to the problem or mystery.

Here's an example. Say a space alien showed up at your school. It wants help getting back home to a planet you've never heard of. What events would take place in the beginning of the story? Right, the alien showing up, kids maybe a little scared at first, and you learn about the alien's dilemma. He probably doesn't speak your language—that's another problem!

How about the middle? Maybe one kid wants to hurt the alien. Others are trying to speak to him. One kid is so terrified he calls 911. The problem becomes clearer—the alien needs to be home before sunrise, or he'll be in danger. What sort of danger? No one is sure, but this is one frightened alien. And he's hungry—but he doesn't seem to eat your sort of food.

The end of the story would describe how everything was resolved. Maybe the alien got home. Maybe he was adopted and stayed on Earth. Maybe he turned into something else. We'll never know until the author tells us.

You Try It!

Take a look at these short stories. They are missing either a beginning, middle, or end. See if you can come up with the part that is missing. What could be the middle of this story, "Harry's Jumpy Brother"? Use your wildest imagination. Then compare your idea with your classmates'.

BEGINNING *Every morning at exactly six o'clock, Harry's little brother, Sam, woke him up by jumping on the bed. No matter how many times Harry told Sam, "Please don't jump on my bed! It makes me seasick!" Sam just went ahead and leaped. It didn't just make Harry seasick. It also rattled his dreams right out of his head. It shook his bones, and it gave him a gigantic headache. What could he do? One day Harry had a plan.*

NO MIDDLE Before you write the middle, read the ending.

END *The next morning Harry woke with a start. No one else was in the room. Just Harry. No one was jumping on the bed and rattling his brains or shaking his dreams. He wasn't seasick at all. In fact, Harry felt absolutely wonderful. His room was totally quiet, with just a thin stream of sunlight coming through the blinds. Harry glanced at the clock. It was eight o'clock, and Sam hadn't come in! His plan had worked. Smiling, Harry got out of bed. His brother wasn't such a bad little kid after all. Maybe Harry would even treat him to ice cream today. But first he had to scramble, or he'd be late for school!*

Does the ending give you any clues as to what might have happened in the middle? Right, it tells us that Harry had a plan and that it worked. To write the middle, you'd need to describe the plan and how Harry put it into action. Maybe it didn't even work the first time—that's up to you.

Now that you've had practice figuring out the middle of "Harry's Jumpy Brother," read the beginning and middle of "The Room at the Top of the Stairs." Then try to think of an ending.

BEGINNING *Nat was bored at his Aunt Sally's house. He had to stay there all summer while his parents toured Europe with their famous kazoo band. So his parents were off having fun, and he was stuck in the country with nothing but bugs and slugs and his very old aunt for company. Nat was a city boy. Bugs and slugs definitely weren't his thing.*

"Remember, stay out of the room at the top of the stairs!" Aunt Sally ordered him as she left for her weekly canasta game. "And no cookies until after dinner. I counted them."

Nat rolled his eyes. Another fun-filled day. He watched a movie. Then he played some games on his computer. Of course his aunt didn't have Internet access. He was about to fix himself a sandwich when he heard strange noises, like somebody gargling.

MIDDLE *Nat followed the sound, up the stairs, a little to the left . . . and suddenly he was right in front of the room at the top of the stairs—the one his aunt told him to stay out of. He heard the sound again, louder now.*

"Hello, anyone in there?" Nat called, knocking gently on the door. He had never believed in ghosts, but suddenly he wasn't so sure. What did you do if you saw a ghost? How were you supposed to act? What should you say?

Nat was sure he heard something bumping around. More gurgley, growly noises. Hands shaking, he slowly turned the knob. All the noises stopped. There was a funny smell. He pushed the door open a crack, then a little wider—and at least 17 cats came streaking out of the room and down the stairs. And there were more inside! He slammed the door and leaned against it. Now what?

NO END What happened next? How would you end this story? Try to come up with some unusual ideas.

Finally, read the middle of "Marley's Mistakes." When you have finished, see if you can come up with a beginning and an end.

NO BEGINNING Read on to find what happens.

MIDDLE *When Marley got to school, everyone was wearing a rainbow-striped shirt. Everyone, that is, except for her. Her shirt was bright red. Actually, it was a blouse. With a collar. She pretty much hated it. Glumly she slunk into class. "Hey, Marley, where's your rainbow shirt?" her friend Tammy asked. "We were all supposed to wear them today! We're going to be on TV!"*

Marley didn't even answer. She felt like a jerk. She stuck out so much in social studies that Mr. Brookbender called on her ten times more than on any other day. When she got to the cafeteria, she couldn't even find Tammy. All she could see was a sea of striped T-shirts. Marley decided she wasn't hungry anymore. Maybe instead of eating, she'd just grab her bike and ride home to get her shirt. Yeah! That's what she'd do. No one would be there, but she had her key.

Marley hopped on her bike and took off. She was sure no one had noticed. It was only four minutes to her house. She'd be back in no time, right? Down Willow Street, around the corner on Grove Street, to Perkins Place. Turn left and there was home! There was an old van parked in front that said Ken Sparks, Electrician. *That was weird. And why was the back door wide open? Marley ran in without thinking. That was her second mistake.*

NO END What do you think happened? Keep the title in mind as you write the beginning and end of this story.

Getting Your Readers' Attention

When you compose or write your story, you want to pull your readers in right from the start with a great opener. You can do this in several different ways.

1. **Start with some action.**

Get your characters moving or doing something interesting. Maybe someone is racing home on his bike in the rainy dusk, already an hour late for dinner. You'd probably want to know what was going on. What kinds of stories might unfold if they started like this?

- Two kids take a shortcut through a farmer's field and are now being chased by a bull.

- A girl is running from a burning house, grabbing three frightened kittens as she leaves. But then she remembers their mother.

- A boy and a nautical robot have discovered the undersea wreck of an old treasure galleon, but the boy's oxygen supply is critically low.

2. Start with compelling dialogue.

"Help! Somebody please help me!" Beth cried.

"One more word out of you, and I'll be sure you stay quiet," growled the thug, as he tightened his grip on Beth's arm.

Wouldn't you want to keep reading if a story started like that? Opening dialogue that raises questions about what's happening gets your readers' attention.

Opening dialogue can also show emotion or provide exciting information:

"I've never been so scared in my life!" Frank cried.

"This will be the first time anyone has set foot on the planet Zyron," Captain Anderson told his exhausted crew.

3. Start with a vivid description.

Give your readers something to visualize right from the start.

For one thousand years, the town of Lester had been under water. But overnight the lake had suddenly dried up. And that morning people woke to find a perfect little colonial village where the swimming hole had been the day before.

Or you might describe an interesting person.

Leo Larson was seven feet tall, and all the townspeople were afraid of him. Maybe it was his angry scowl. Maybe it was his hair that looked like barbed wire. Maybe it was because no one ever saw him without his miserable, drooling mutt, Loofah. Actually, Leo and Loofah looked a lot alike.

You Try It!

See if you can come up with three great openings using first action, then dialogue, and finally description.

CHAPTER 2

Who's the Story About? Creating Characters

Characters Aren't Just People!

The characters in a story can be people, animals, or sometimes even things. Not all characters are equally important. Usually there are only one or two main characters. The main character, sometimes called a protagonist, is the character who's most fully developed. Readers learn about him or her in lots of ways: by what he says, thinks, or does; by what she wears or looks like; by what other characters say; and so on. As a writer you work hard to acquaint your readers with your main characters. This helps readers relate to them so they get really involved in your story.

Think about your favorite books or stories. Chances are they've had some memorable characters. *Harriet the Spy*, by Louise Fitzhugh, is about a smart young girl who tries to make sense of her life and the people around her by writing about them in a notebook. She's spying on others to try to understand both their lives and her own. But when her classmates find her notebook and read the entries aloud, they are horrified that Harriet has recorded their secrets, and they get really angry. Harriet becomes an outcast, but her creativity and resourcefulness help her solve the problem and save the day for herself.

In *Sounder* the oldest son tells the story, but Sounder, the family hound, is the only character with a name. When the father is jailed for taking a hog to feed his family, life is turned upside down. The boy's strong desire to learn to read and his struggle to help his family all make for an unforgettable character. In some ways, because he has no name, he represents all children who have struggled to overcome and succeed.

Because of Winn-Dixie, by Kate DiCamillo, is full of wonderful characters. Ten-year-old Opal yearns to know ten things about her mother, who has abandoned her. She showers Winn-Dixie, a scruffy stray dog, with love. With her dog's help, Opal learns that it doesn't matter what people did in the past. What really matters is who they are and what they do now.

Memorable characters are no accident. Authors took time and care to make them that way, helping readers to not only "see" the character but also to know what's important to the character—what makes him or her cry or laugh, or get mad or scared. Creating well-developed characters takes time. Where do you start? Do you just think of a character like a big, tall man with a mustache? Well, no.

Think about a character who wants or needs something badly, or who has a big problem. A boy wants to find and help a friend. A girl needs to win the talent show in order to get the prize money to help her family. If he or she doesn't succeed, disaster could strike. The goal should be difficult to achieve, which sets up the conflict. A character wanting a glass of water doesn't count, unless that character is out in the desert dying of thirst!

So what else might a character want? In *The Wizard of Oz*, by L. Frank Baum, Dorothy and her assorted odd friends want to go to Oz to ask the Wizard for things like a brain, a heart, and courage. Dorothy just wants to go home! There are all sorts of obstacles to their journey. People who try to stop characters from meeting their goals are called antagonists, because they create conflict with the protagonist. The Wicked Witch, for example, wants to stop Dorothy and her friends—she is an antagonist. In the end, Dorothy learns that she had the power to go home all along, that it was right on her feet. She also learns about what is important in life, like love and friendship—and that there's no place like home. *Holes,* by Louis Sachar, is full of great characters, too. The men who run the work camp want to stop the kids from escaping, so they are the antagonists.

Jess is the main character in *Bridge to Terabithia*, by Katherine Paterson. Jess struggles to impress his classmates, please his father, and find his place in the world. He loves to draw, but being an artist isn't exactly valued on the farm. His parents need him to be able to care for the animals, plow the land, and work hard. Going to museums doesn't really factor in to that. Then he meets a new girl from the ritzy suburbs. Her friendship and lively imagination show him an inner strength he never knew existed. Together they build a castle stronghold in a secret kingdom that they alone rule. Jess becomes a wiser, more understanding person as a result of their friendship.

You Try It!

Think of a character that wants to achieve something. Then list three or four reasons why this goal is really difficult to achieve. Here's an example.

Maya is a terrific swimmer. She wants to train for the Olympics. What stands in her way?

- She doesn't have much racing experience.

- She lives in an area where there is only one public pool. It is always really crowded.

- She doesn't have a coach.

- Her parents think her idea is foolish because it is too expensive to use the pool in town. They want her to concentrate on her schoolwork.

Here are some ways Maya can try to get around these obstacles.

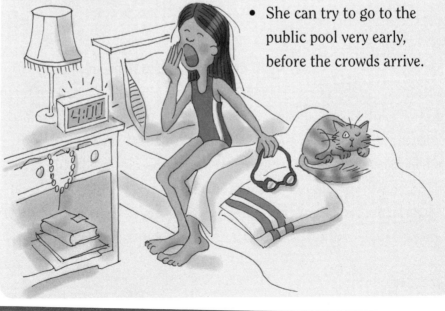

- She can try to go to the public pool very early, before the crowds arrive.

- She can take lessons and join a swim team, if she can find one close by.

- She can ask around to see if there is a swimming coach at the pool who might like to take her on.

- She can move to her aunt's town where there is an organized swimming program and live with her aunt while she trains.

Remember, the more you tell readers about your characters, the more interesting they will be. You can describe how characters feel by their actions. Show them sobbing when they are sad, or running when they are frightened, or even breaking things in anger. How might you show that a character is nervous? A character can *say* how he or she is feeling, as in *"I feel terrible."* But characters can also *think* about their feelings and *reflect* how they feel: *Mary was so miserable that she wanted to hide under her bed for the rest of the year.*

Think About Dialogue.

Be sure your characters talk! Readers learn a great deal about characters through both what they say and what others say to and about them.

- *"I hate dragons! I am determined to slay every one of them! No dragon is safe around me!" trumpeted Morgan the Magnificent.* (We know that this character is loud and boastful, and we know what he wants.)

- *"Wait, don't shut off the light! Ghosts might come in! Maybe there's one in the closet!" wailed Megan.* (We know that this character is scared and anxious and that she believes in ghosts.)

- *"Why am I so shy? I hate it! What's wrong with me?" cried Katelyn.* (We know how this character feels about herself.)

- *"Don't ever tell Daniel anything—he totally can't keep a secret," Tim whispered.* (We know how this character feels about another one.)

How characters respond to different situations can be revealing, too. A wishy-washy character will hold back. A strong character will go after what he or she wants. For example, perhaps Morgan the Magnificent takes archery lessons to help him slay the dragons. This shows that he really means business. Perhaps Megan decides to leave the lights on and to keep the dog on her bed for the night. This makes her feel safe, and it shows that Megan is determined and resourceful.

Sometimes what other people say or how they respond gives us more information about a character.

- *"Morgan the Magnificent is a terrible dragon hunter. The only person who thinks he's magnificent is him!" say the townspeople. "There's no way he'll ever slay a single dragon."* (This creates more tension for Morgan and makes him need or want to prove himself. It also tells us that he might not be as fabulous as he seems to think he is.)

- *"You're a big baby!" Megan's little brother, Alex, taunted her.* (This reflects conflict between Megan and her little brother, who seems to feel he is braver, though younger. Who will turn out to be the courageous one?)

It's fine to use the word *said* with dialogue, but there are plenty of other interesting verbs you can use, too. Words like *cried, sighed, argued,* and *pleaded* add to a reader's understanding of the situation. You can also use adverbs to pep up your dialogue. A character can say something calmly or excitedly or angrily—and that can change the whole meaning of what he or she is saying. Different verbs can completely change the way in which you visualize the following dialogue.

- *"I hate cheese," said Bob calmly.*
- *"I hate cheese!" screamed Bob.*
- *"I hate cheese," Bob whispered.*
- *"I hate cheese!" giggled Bob.*
- *"I hate cheese," muttered Bob, as he tried to scrape it off his pizza.*

Sometimes you don't need to attribute a line of dialogue to anyone if there are only two speakers. In the following dialogue, you can easily pick out which lines are Sam's and which are Maggie's.

"Can you puh-leeze lend me ten dollars?" Maggie begged.

"Forget it," snapped Sam. "Last time I did that, you lost it."

"It won't happen again."

"Yes, it will!"

"No, it won't! I promise."

"No way."

You Try It!

Using colorful verbs and adverbs, write dialogue for one or more of the following situations.

- Two people are arguing about whose dog is smarter.

- A girl is lost in the woods. She meets a unicorn that tries to tell her how to get home.

- A boy tries to convince his parents that he is mature enough to stay home alone for the evening. They aren't buying it.

Think About Names

What's in a name? Sometimes quite a bit. What would a boy named Bartholomew Beeswatter be like? Can you visualize him? What do you see? What about someone named Mrs. Agnes Applebug or Sir Reginald Newton Charleston III? How would you describe a cat named Spike? A dog named Marshmallow Fluffy? Think of good names for the following characters.

- A boy who asks questions all the time about absolutely everything, which drives people crazy

- A girl who loves to dance and does it constantly

- A man who makes and sells cheese for a living

- An old woman who lives alone with her pets—a skunk and a boa constrictor (name all three of them)

You Try It!

Create a complete character from top to bottom. Use the following guidelines to help you. You might not use all this information if you are writing a story, but thinking deeply about your main character(s) makes for more interesting characterization.

- What is your character's name?

- What does your character look like?

- Describe your character's personality.

- Where does the character live?

- Describe the character's bedroom.

- Describe the character's pets.

- What kind of family does the character have?

- How does your character like to dress?

- What is his or her favorite food?

- What does your character like to do in his or her spare time?

- What does your character want?

- What is your character's main problem?

- What's most important for readers to know about your character?

- Anything else?

CHAPTER 3

Where Am I? Creating Settings

Another Place, Another Time

The setting tells when and where a story takes place. In other words, it's a location in time and place. The setting can be Africa or Kansas, a tiny room or a huge castle. It can be in the next century, or 3,000 years ago. Settings are more important in some stories than in others. *Bridge to Terabithia*, for example, takes place in a rural setting. The woods in the story are crucial to the plot. Changing the setting would change the entire story.

Could you imagine *The Wizard of Oz* taking place in your hometown? Probably not. Oz is a rare and magical place, and few hometowns fit that description. Describe your settings as fully as you can. Your reader should be able to picture both characters *and* settings.

You Try It!

Describe each setting so that readers can visualize it.

- A cave-man's dwelling
- An enchanted rain forest
- A day-care center on Jupiter in the year 2080
- A present-day dessert restaurant in a large city

Names can tell you a lot about a setting. What do you think the following places are like?

- Planet Hexahedron
- Ginnie Mae's Perfect Pancake House
- Sea World Hotel
- Big Bad Bob's Bison Ranch

Now try to come up with names for the following places.

- A dry, dusty town in the American West
- A gym and spa for dogs and cats
- A volcanic island newly risen in the Pacific
- A forest in Africa where dinosaurs still live

Sometimes the setting presents challenges to the characters. Remember the girl who wanted to be an Olympic swimmer but who lived in a landlocked area with only one public pool? That makes her goal tougher to meet, doesn't it? If she lived in an area with lots of lakes, there might be less of a problem. Depending on your story, you don't have to limit yourself to a real setting. If you're writing a fable or fantasy or science fiction, you can invent your own world!

Use these guidelines to give it a try.

- What's the name of your fantasy world?

- What is life like here?

- Who rules this world?

- What is the climate like?

- What are the laws of this world? What happens if you break them?

- What holidays are celebrated here?

- What do people look like?

- What do they eat?

- What do people do for fun?

- What kinds of jobs do people have?

- What colors are in this world?

- What animals exist here? Pets?

- Would you like it here? Why or why not? And if not, how would you leave?

Once you have your characters and your setting, you'll be ready to focus on your plot—the series of events that make up your story.

CHAPTER 4

What's Happening? Creating the Plot

What Is a Plot Exactly?

The series of events that happen in a story is called the plot. You can have a wonderful bunch of characters and a descriptive setting, but without an interesting plot, your readers won't stick with your story. Most good plots involve a problem or conflict that the main character is facing and the eventual solution. Solving a mystery counts as solving a problem. Sometimes there are even subplots—separate stories within the story. But there is always one main plot that shapes the narrative. Plots can be broken down into five components: exposition, rising action, climax, falling action, and resolution. Sometimes it helps to picture an arc, like this:

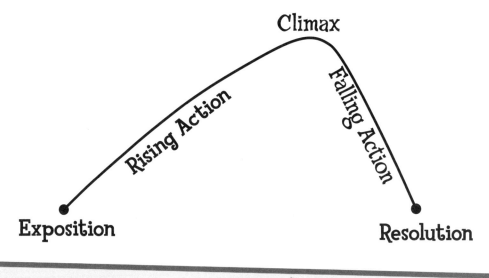

Notice that the climax does *not* come right in the middle. It's more near the end. There's a good reason for that. What do you think it is? Let's take a look at each point on the arc.

EXPOSITION This is the beginning of the story. We meet the characters, get a sense of the setting, and are introduced to the problem or conflict that the character faces. These problems need to be major enough to build a good story on. For example, if Dana's problem is that she can't wake up on time to catch the school bus, that's probably not enough to carry a whole story. The solution is too easy—an alarm clock. However, will she be able to save a neighbor's dog that she knows is being badly mistreated? This problem has a lot at stake. The outcome could be happy, or it could be tragic. It has the makings of a great story.

In Judy Blume's *Tales of a Fourth Grade Nothing*, for example, the exposition introduces us to Peter Hatcher; his turtle, Dribble; and his little brother, Fudge. We learn that Peter's family lives in New York City and that his father is in advertising. We get a sense right away that Fudge is an accident just waiting to happen.

RISING ACTION In rising action we learn more about the problem or conflict that the character is trying to resolve. Rising action is the series of events that build suspense and make you want to keep reading. As an author you develop the problem with more details. Rising action takes a while—you don't spill all the details at once. For example, the girl could tell her parents about the mistreated dog. But her parents could explain that it isn't her business, that

everyone trains dogs differently, and that the owner is not someone they want to confront. (Hmm. What does that tell you about the owner?) The girl sees the situation getting worse, and she gathers her courage to face the neighbor. But instead of heeding the girl's plea to be kinder to the dog, the neighbor tells her to mind her own business. He becomes even meaner to the dog.

In *Tales of a Fourth Grade Nothing*, the rising action introduces us to some of Peter's and Fudge's friends. We also read more about Peter's relationship to Fudge and Fudge's various mishaps and antics. Many people find Fudge funny and adorable, but Peter is not one of them.

CLIMAX This is the point at which the problem or complication reaches its peak. Readers may feel the most riveted here because they don't know what is going to happen, but something's got to give. The climax is a turning point. Maybe the neighbor becomes so mean that he chains the dog to his workbench without food or water because the dog has been disobedient. The girl frees the dog and hides it in her garage, nursing it to health. All the while, the neighbor is searching for it and threatening the girl. The neighbor discovers his dog and confronts the girl in her garage—her parents are not at home, and no one else is around. Perhaps the neighbor has a weapon or finds one in the garage.

The climax of *Tales of a Fourth Grade Nothing* would be when Fudge swallows Dribble. He is carted off to the hospital in an ambulance for Dribble retrieval.

FALLING ACTION In falling action we see the effect of the climax on the characters. As the plot moves toward a resolution, each character responds differently to what happened in the climax. While rising action is drawn out and builds slowly to a climax, falling action "falls" more quickly. Things move to an ending because the tension has been released and you're ready to find out how it all works out. Perhaps the dog defends the girl from the wrath of its owner, since the girl has been kind and earned the love and trust of the dog. The dog might actually threaten its owner, who might then realize what has happened and how he is responsible.

In *Tales of a Fourth Grade Nothing*, this would be when the doctors succeed in getting the turtle out of Fudge. Fudge gets lots of attention, and Peter is now without a pet. He feels sad and resentful.

RESOLUTION The problem or conflict is resolved, or the mystery is solved. Perhaps the neighbor sees his dog is now healthy and happy, and sees how brave the girl has been. The solution could be that the neighbor vows to take better care of his dog and hires the girl to walk the dog every day. Or he could give his dog to the girl and ask to visit periodically. He might even breed the dog and give the girl a puppy.

The resolution in *Tales of a Fourth Grade Nothing* occurs when Peter's father brings home a dog for Peter. Peter names his new pet Turtle.

Here's another example of plot structure.

EXPOSITION It's the week of the finals in the basketball tournament. Zack's team has made it into the finals, but just barely. They need serious practice in order to beat their archrivals. When Zack hears strange noises in the locker room equipment closet one night after practice, he wonders what's up. Zack's not supposed to go into the closet without permission, but clearly something's going on in there! What can he do?

RISING ACTION Determined to be bold, Zack enlists the help of his best friend. They go into the closet and discover that all the basketballs are missing. Zack notices a broken neon green shoelace. The only person he knows who wears green shoelaces is this new kid, Roger, but he's not on the team. Is Roger working for the other team? Why would he do that? Where could he take 18 basketballs? Then Roger goes missing.

CLIMAX After a long search, and without much help from anyone, Zack finds Roger, who is living alone in a beat-up trailer with his pet black snake. Roger has a father, but he's absent as often as he's around. No one knew. Upset because he hadn't made the team, Roger was trying to even the score. Now, embarrassed that Zack knows about his miserable situation, Roger gets even more desperate. He grabs Zack's bike and takes off, leaving Zack and the snake locked in the trailer.

FALLING ACTION After several days of frantic activity, both Zack and Roger are released or located. They meet and talk. Roger leads Zack to the basketballs. Roger agrees to return them in person.

RESOLUTION Roger apologizes to the team. Zack privately tells the coach about Roger's sad situation. The coach invites Roger to join the team for practices and try out again next year. But when Roger's father shows up from wherever he's been, Roger has to leave the team and his new friends and try to make it in some new school. Everyone on the team wishes him well, and they go on to win the tournament. Roger is there to cheer them on.

You Try It!

Write a story outline. Be sure to indicate the problem or conflict, rising action, climax, falling action, and resolution. Use a form similar to the diagram on page 34. Remember that there is more happening in the rising action than there is in the falling action. Then write a rough draft of your story.

CHAPTER 5

Finishing Touches

Revising and Editing

You've finally completed a rough draft. Your opening is strong, your rising action is interesting and well paced, you have a tense climax, and a knockout ending. The basics are all in place. Now is the time for finishing touches.

The revising and editing stage is the part of the story-writing process where you perfect and refine your work. All writers, even famous ones, revise their work. They know that each time they do, the story is going to get better. In your second, third, or even fourth draft, you polish what you have written and maybe even add to it.

Here's a short checklist to guide you as you fine-tune your work.

1. Read over your story, read it to a friend, or have a friend read it. Look for places where you can add descriptive words. Can you visualize your characters and settings? Would readers know what they look like? Think about taste, touch, sight, sound, and smell. Adjectives help create strong images, like a *ferocious* dog, a *glistening* snake, or a *gooey, cheesy* pizza. Adverbs show action more clearly, like a boy running *fiercely*, or a girl chewing *thoughtfully*.

2. Get to know similes and metaphors. A simile makes a comparison using *like* or *as*. She was as pretty as a blooming rose. He had a serve like a rocket blasting off. A metaphor makes a comparison without *like* or *as*. His mom was a busy bee. As she ran, Leslie was a bird in flight. Similes and metaphors are handy ways to describe characters and settings.

3. Read your dialogue out loud. Can you make it more natural? Remember to add words like *cried, argued,* and *whispered* to help give a sense of how characters sound and feel.

4. Look over the conflict, rising action, climax, falling action, and resolution. This is the arc of the story. Does it make sense? Are the transitions smooth and logical, or are things awkwardly stuck together? Does one story event seem to follow another naturally, or do things seem disjointed? Is the ending satisfying or is it a total coincidence? Your plot should be believable, even if it is fantasy. Once your readers enter your world, whatever it is, the events of the plot need to make sense within that world.

5. Writers often get reviews or critiques of their work. Reviews point out what is good about a story and what is weak. Imagine a review of your story. Is the plot exciting? The dialogue compelling? What about the main characters?

Here's a checklist you can use to make sure everything's in good shape.

☐ My story makes the reader want to keep reading to the end.

☐ Readers can picture the characters from my descriptions.

☐ My characters seem real.

☐ Readers can picture the setting from my description.

☐ I have a problem or conflict in my story.

☐ The plot reaches a clear climax.

☐ The problem is solved at the end of the story.

☐ The solution to the problem is believable.

☐ The writing sounds as if I am talking to the reader.

☐ I like what I have written.

I hope you've discovered just how much fun writing stories can be. You've learned how to start your stories with a bang and how to create a character that seems to walk right off the page. You know how to write compelling dialogue and why the setting can sometimes be as important as the character you're writing about. You've learned how to craft a story that builds to a climax and that keeps readers interested. Stories teach us about ourselves, about others, and about the world. There are many stories out there waiting to be told. I bet some of them will be yours.

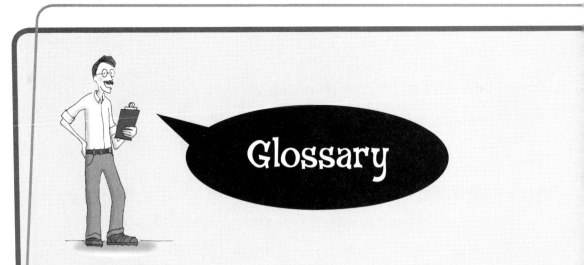

Glossary

Antagonist

The antagonist is the character in a story that works against the main character, or protagonist. This provides conflict. The antagonist may be a person or persons, but can also be a concept or an idea.

Character

Any person or being in a story is a character. Characters carry the action of the story, help the protagonist or antagonist, or simply influence or participate in the plot in some way.

Climax

The climax comes near the end of the story. It occurs when the rising action of the plot reaches a peak, and something has to give. The climax is usually a tense, amazing moment in the story. It is followed by falling action and resolution.

Conflict

The conflict is the struggle that characters face and work to overcome in a story. Conflict is usually at the center of the plot. It provides suspense and tension in the story. Conflict is not always one person against another. Sometimes characters are in conflict with themselves, with nature, or with society.

Dialogue

Dialogue is the spoken words in a story. Conversations between characters are called dialogue.

Draft

A first draft is a rough first attempt at writing a story. As you edit and revise your writing, you may create a second, third, or even tenth draft before you are satisfied with the final result. Each draft is a revision that attempts to improve on the draft you wrote before.

Edit

To edit is to correct and improve writing. When you edit a story, you check for errors in grammar, spelling, and punctuation. You also work to improve the overall piece by adding details, transitions, and effective vocabulary.

Exposition

Exposition includes the beginning stage of a story. It supplies details about characters and setting, and introduces the conflict or problem that will be at the heart of the story. An exposition can be one brief passage or several longer ones. It may also be called the introduction.

Falling Action

Falling action includes everything that happens after the climax, up to the resolution. Usually after the climax, characters are changed in some way. Falling action describes the consequences of the climax and its effect on the characters.

Genre

A category of literature, such as fantasy, that has particular characteristics in common. Also called *text type*.

Introduction

An introduction sets up a story by presenting the characters, setting, and potential problem or conflict. Another word for introduction is *exposition*.

Metaphor

A metaphor is one form of figurative language. It is a way of describing something using a direct comparison. For example, *the wind's gentle fingers combed her hair as tulips in bright tutus danced in the breeze.*

Plot

The plot is the sum of all the events of a story. It is made up of the conflict, rising action, climax, falling action and resolution. The plot usually revolves around a problem or conflict that is solved or settled at the end of the story.

Protagonist

The protagonist is the main character. The protagonist has to confront the major conflict or solve the problem in a story.

Red Herring

A red herring is a fake clue usually found in a mystery. A red herring is meant to mislead or distract the reader so that the more important clues are not noticed or so that the outcome isn't easy to predict.

Resolution

Resolution is how the problem or conflict of the story is resolved or worked out. All the loose ends of the plot are tied up in the resolution. Sometimes in the resolution, a character will have learned something new or will have changed in some way.

Revision

Revision is part of editing. This occurs when writers revisit a story to fix things that are confusing, unclear, boring, or awkward.

Rising Action

Rising action includes all of the events of a plot that lead to the climax. Rising action builds suspense. Usually the reader does not know what's coming or how a story will end.

Setting

Setting is where and when a story takes place. The setting fixes a story in time and place to help the reader enter that world.

Simile

A simile is a form of figurative language that compares two things using the words *like* or *as*. For example, *she sings like a bird*, or *he is as fast as a speeding bullet*.

Subplot

A subplot is like a secondary story that is less important than the main plot. For example, if the plot is about a king who was taken captive by an evil giant, the subplot might be the story of how his wife managed back home at the castle, taking care of the kingdom.